The
Tao
Poems

Dwight Cavanagh

Print information available on the last page

Rev. date: 09/11/2018

To order additional copies of this book, contact:
Xlibris
1-888-795-4274
www.Xlibris.com
Orders@Xlibris.com

Dedication

To Lynnie, Catie,
and Joseph with love
and
To all Michael Students
wherever extant

Table of Contents

Cover Illustration and Frontspiece:
Original Japanese wood-block snow print by Hokusui of the
Duck Pond at Ryoaň-ji Zen Temple in Kyoto, circa 1860 from
the collection of the author. The view of the leaning pine tree
and pond remain nearly unchanged today.

BASHŌ

Cloud Casting
Sudden
    raindrop.

Life Plan
    Day's task.

Tranquil Path
Safe to Sea

7-22-92[1]

THE WAY

The Way to Tao
Runs through a pathless land;
No dogmae, nor formulae
DIRECT THE FATE OF MAN;
But each morning clear
and without fear,
A CALM I AM.

2-01-93[2]

MARKINGS

We will meet again
Before the end,
To drink the Cup of Sighs
for might have been.

Then sweet shared joy
Our single pains shall mend
And in Essence time
Shall blend
Then rest and try again.

02-02-93
07-02-04

SIGNS

Today I saw a bluebird
The first sure sign of spring.
Heard the tree frogs by the pond
and the crickets sing.
Though winter's snows
are deep and cold
And cruel Jack Frost is King
Yet deep the Easter Lily sleeps
And lives to come again.

02-02-93

WU-WEI

Let go.
Let be.
Let flow.
Go free.

11-04-94[3]

L'Envoi

When the last hope has broken,
And the last fear is dead;
When the last word is spoken,
And the last prayer is said;
With no anticipation
With no desire nor dread,
Rest at the end of action,
With the final lesson read.

12-05-94

EVENSONG

Tao, thank you for this day,
For the love of the LIGHT,
For the grace of the WAY,
In the joy of the PLAY,
And a sleep on the night.

11-9-95

TOLKIEN CHANNELS

Five inner eyes for
*   artisan souls;*
Three for the Magi Sage
*   in halls of stone;*
Two for young zealot priest;
One for server acolyte
*   and Warrior-Kings on*
*   guardian throne.*
One LIGHT to rule them all,
One LIGHT to find them,
One LIGHT to bring them all,
And in the TAØ bind them.

01-10-96[4]

HERACLITUS' SONG

ethos anthropoi daimon

Nothing is wasted.
No lesson is lost.
The daimon once visaged
Is not slain by fear's cost.
All choices are mutile.
Each path is right.
No life is futile.
All lead to the LIGHT.

03-11-96 (1)[5]
09-13-01 (2)

SYNCHRONICITY

In each life's daily task
Nothing ever is by chance;
Order wears a Chaos Mask
In the Nata Rāja's Dance.

03-12-96 [6, 7]

TAŌ

Polarity is the tension
within meaning
Music is the silence
between the notes.
The WAY is oft glimpsed
dreaming,
Midst the seeming of
illusions hoax.

03-15-96 [8]

ENFIN . . .

Quand, je vrai trouve,
Je vrai jouet;
Quand, je me reste,
J'etude vrai.

03-15-96

ZAZEN

No Anger,
No Hate.
No Fear
No Fate.

05-10-96 [9]

Cycles

Nothing is forever;
    All seasons turn at last.
Even the weariest NEVER
    Moves on to forget the
      past.
And with TIME and times
      forgotten,
Fresh chances rise begotten
And cadence by cadence
A new PLAY is cast.

07-08-96

The Furies
Tissiphone, Maegara, Alecto

All anger flows from
Expectations;
Typhoon's fury rises
From thermal sea.
Joy comes from inner
Relaxation,
In letting go and
Letting be.

7- 17,-96 [10]

Teilhard

In Awareness Being,
To Becoming Flowing,
In each choosing Seeing,
To evolving Knowing.

02-21-97 [11]

PASCHAL
Il Fait Jouet

To always see how,
To never know why,
Some things live
Yet others die.
To only be NOW
And everyday try.

06-25-97 [12]
St. William's Day

J.S. ROUNDS BACH

Once we see the GAME,
We no longer wish to play,
Nothing remains the same,
Not for a single day.

Once we see the PLAY,
Life's no longer a willing game,
Not for a single day,
Is anything the same.

Not for a single DAY
Is anything the same;
Once we see the PLAY
We long to quit the GAME.

PROUST
Le recherché du temps perdu

There are few who now remember here,
Hot tears and Angst of bygone fear;
The saddest thoughts of all our sin:
Might not have been, should not have been.
But ever the WAY leads up and on.
Past times and faces and choices are gone.
And we must trust the PATTERN weft
As ever yet the WEAVER weaves,
Of hope and fear become bereft
And only the love of the PLAY perceive.

11-18-98 [13]

Tê
"action without doing"
Lao-Tse

Like a tree .... BE
Like water .... FLOW
In darkness .... SEE
Hold fast in .... LETTING GO

11-20-98 [14]

KARMA

When anger wounds with
    hammer blows,
The choices of the weaving
    wheel;
Then Clotho in reflection sews
Ribbons that must be burned to
    heal.

07-08-99 [15,16]

RIBBONS

Not for minor matters
Are Clotho's ribbons made;
Only for choices shattered
Are Karma's debts repaid.

The choices knit the pattern
Each thread exceeding fine;
But there is no trade
Or excuses made
That will cancel a twist of line.

07-09-99 [16]
10-14-04

PRAJNA

On the shining Pearl of
        KNOWLEDGE,
The Dragon must yet discern.
The seamless edge of WISDOM
Where Good and Evil join.

07-09-99 [17]

C'EST TOUT

For today,
Learn and Play,
Do your Best;
LAUGH with Zest,
Live the WAY;
Night's for rest.

09-17-99

THE BUTTERFLY'S SONG

Joy without holding,
No choice is wrong;
Ever unfolding,
The butterfly's song.

Love without scolding,
Each choice is right;
Ever enfolding,
The song is the LIGHT.

06-23-00
06-18-03

MONADS

The few against the many,
The big against the small,
Honor bound to dishonor,
The TAO tests them all.

Cast from choice of SEVEN
Each bound with life to dwell.
With no Hell or Heaven
But only MAYA's spell.

No one cares who loses,
And no one counts who wins.
FATE scores no supposes
But only KARMA's sins.

LOVE is the only LESSON.
Learn it and you can go.
Free from fear and reason
In MAYA's puppet show.

07-26-04 [18-20]

LETHĒ

Free from Judgement and Judges
From Malice and lawyers who steal,
From the pain of long-held grudges,
Whose hurt was never real,
From too much love of striving,
From vengeful fears set free,
I thank with High Thanksgiving,
The Eternal THREE that be;
That every life plan closes,
When there are no more supposes,
And letting go of poses,
We each at last go free.

11-16-97 [21]

RETREAT

When I am tired and down
Fed up with WRONG and RIGHT,
I cast away my frown,
And open the EYE OF LIGHT,
Of LIGHT and LOVE and
        LAUGHTER,
Glad tears in flowing streams,
With no more EVER AFTER,
And only a dream of DREAMS.

05-18/19-01 [22]

CHOICES

At the crossroads NEVER
The road forks left to WELL,
Bye the lane to MAYBE,
And down the knoll to SHALL;
Across the river SADNESS,
Over the Bridge REGRET,
Through the village FORGIVENESS,
And sleep at the Inn FORGET.

06-04-01

Je Ne regret Rien
pour Edith Piaf

My candle's burned to smatters
It shall not last the night,
But that no longer matters
For yet its flame is bright.

All I have is a sword
And a fight I can not win
But can not stay from fighting
Or yet go home again.

Now my sword has shattered.
I can not hold back the night.
But that no longer matters
For I have served the LIGHT.

02-12-04 [23]

MAYA

Here, we art come born to
stare
At each other passing fair;
But we can not go,
'Til we know,
Never is another there.

01-12-04 [20]

CENTERS

On rhythm's drums
Words dance.
Knowledge Comes
As by chance.

In stillness free
Thoughts flow.
First to BE.
Then to KNOW.

06-18-02 [24]

AMAZING GRACE

Tiny gay wildflowers grow
In the unexpected place;
With still presence there to show
Sudden, sure and silent grace.

06-18-02

JERUSALEM

There are two roads to heaven
One by loving laughter led;
The other has pain for leaven,
And with fear and hate is tread.

The bane of fear is laughter
And true joy dismisses fate
But Hell swift follows after
With HOPE replaced by HATE.

08-13-02

SAMSARA

When attachment rules the head,
Then from Desire's siren wheel,
Clotho spins gossamer thread
Binding bight and bitter steel,
None of which were ever real.

09-09-02

CHURCHILL
IN
KAI-LUNGS GARDEN of
Bright Images

I heard the nightingale of BIWA,
The crashing waves of MISHIMA
    BAY.
Drifted with clouds of FUJISAMA,
Sunlit dancing in blue ASHI's day.

The short words are the clearest,
Still, the old words are the best
That bring the Tao nearest,
And light the daimon's road to rest.

09-12-02$^{25\text{-}29}$

LAO-tze

Not what is seen,
　　Not what is said
Nor what is thought,
　　Or what is read,
The TAØ is not sought or
　　found
But in the silence in the
　　sound.

09-13-02

DAIMON
Robert Frost

Something is in every vine
That climbs a standing wall;
Tho it takes an endless time,
Yet every stone shall fall.

09-13-03[30]

RUBICON
alea jacta est

Now truly are we done.
The dice of fate have run.
Events must take their course.
Not softened by remorse
Nor by fear's costs undone.

01-08-03

Oku-no-HOSOMICHI
A narrow road to the north

Age by step the Daimon tills.
Ever up and never down;
Drop by drop Agape fills
Spills and hallows ETHOS'
ground.

02-08-03

ENOUGH?

Lord, I am tired;
I have done my best.
It is up to you,
To decide what's next,
Or a Time for rest?

03-06/07-03

NUNC DIMITIS

Now our race is ended,
The final tasks are done.
Grace our pain has mended,
The cheering has begun!
Joy has slain depression;
The victory is won!

08-25-03

LECTIO DIVINA

Time and Grace have set me
    free.
All I am and all I see
By the TAØ of the Three.
To become what I must be,
To become what I must be.

08-25-03[31]

SHIRAZ
The place of lions

Loneliness is the sound of rain
Quiet strumming on my window pane
That breaks the stillness of the night
And wakens memories akin to pain.

Loneliness is the sound of quiet
In this dark night far from home
When inner thoughts run riot
And the naked mind is all alone.

Loneliness is the sound of laughter
Lovers passing in the street.
Quiet will come to them hereafter
But dawn to me before I sleep.

Norus, 1973
Shiraz, Iran

J. Prufrock & Co.

If never to be forgotten,
Must we stagnate and
Stay around?
Is existence sole begotten
Not out of sight or out of
sound?

10-30-03

TODAY

You can have Tomorrow,
And I shall take today,
Not the path to sorrow
Where yet the PAST holds
sway.

None from TIME can borrow,
Nor praise and pain repay,
You can have tomorrow,
And I shall have today.

11-14-03

KINDNESS

Each small smile of
   Kindness
With Love our sadness
   mends
And to a soul in darkness
A gleaming beacon sends.

11-14-03

WHERE ARE THOSE . . . ?

Where are those who help people
    One by one
    One by one
And those who stand in the crowd
    and order it done?

Where are those who hurt people
    One by one
    One by one
And those who stand in the steeple
    and order it done?

Where are those who judge people
    One by one
    One by one
And those who stand in the crowd
    And watch it done?

07-02-04

BUNRAKU

We are but shadows dancing
In a shadow puppet PLAY;
Gay laughing, crying, prancing
Banished by the noon of day.

Faster, faster calls the MASTER
Go as fast as you can go.
Follow TRIUMPH and
   DISASTER,
Maya's tricksters in the SHOW.

12-30-03[32]

KAIGEN

When night holds silent laughter
And gone are Sadness and
    Pains,
With no more EVERAFTER,
Nor hope of gold or gains,
Then in the DAIMON MASTER
Only Kaigen remains.

12-30-04[33]

SEASONS

There's times for songs
 and sowing
And times to hide or run,
And time for Judgments owing
When the final playing's done.

09-01-04

NOW

Dragonfly, O Dragonfly
Soaring in the summer sky
O what head or heart or I
Dare tell that tonite you die?

09-01-04

MY SONG

Some sing of sweet sadness,
Or gladness bold and bright,
Of MALICE Mother of MADNESS,
Or FEAR the Father of
NIGHT.

Some paint with bold colors,
Others in black and white.
I paint in simple words
the TAO in the LIGHT.

02-12-04

Nata-Raja

SHIVA, Lord of the Balance,
Treads out the grapes of TIME
And all our Words and Actions
To vinegar or wine.

And when one door closes,
Another opens wide,
From the Law of the Balance
No single soul can hide.

5-05-05

ZEN

Thoughts, words and actions
Well up within the mind;
Bold Shadows Brave
In Plato's Cave
All follow the arrow TIME.

6-15-05

Whatever

Whatever the choice,
No note is wrong.
No discordant voice
Can silence the SONG.

8-19-05

SEVEN

Every Seeker finds the WAY;
Remembering is aons long.
Cadence Cast within the PLAY,
Every fragment knows the SONG,
Every fragment knows the SONG.

12-8-05

INNIGSKEIT
für Ranier Maria Rilke

Slow wind in the eaves,
Snow light in the air,
White dappled on leaves,
Bright burnished and bare:
A PATTERN that WEAVES,
The Daimon perceives
While MAYA deceives
The TAO is there.

5-18-06[34]

NOTES

1. Bashō, Matsuo (1644 – 1698) was a Zen-haiku sensei-master who was also a mendicant-traveling monk. His life was structured by his exterior journeys that covered almost all of Japan. For him, travel itself was the process toward enlightenment; the journey was the destination. His master work is Oku-No-Hosomichi or the "Narrow road that leads to the north," illuminating his external and internal progress by a diary containing Haiku poems. This modus is very similar to that of the late Dag Hammarskjöld (1905-1961), Secretary-General of the United Nations whose posthumously-published diary-poem memoirs are titled, "Markings," and who notes in his own words that "the longest journey is the journey inwards." In both cases, the journey is "process" and the "process is the reality" (A.N. Whitehead).

2. In Greek-influenced Christianity, the "Way" or Logos" (WORD) is personified as the "Christos" or second person of the Trinity. In the TAO, this is the "Inspiration" leaflet of the THREE. (Action, Inspiration, Expression)

3. Wu-Wei (action free of desires, intention or motivation) is the TAØ (Laotzu). This is one of the more significant TAØist influences on the development of Zen Buddhism. Interestingly, in almost identical words: "Let go and let be," it is articulated by Meister Eckhart's sermons to medieval Christians. See also the writings of St. Theresa of Avila and St. John of the Cross (16th century Spain).

4. J.R.R. Tolkien (1892 - 1973) English professor, philologist, and author of "The Lord of the Rings" trilogy.

5. Heraclitus of Cos (ca. 500 BC), Greek philosopher. A study of the commentary by Roger Van Deck, "Expect the unexpected

(or you won't find it) (Free Press, NY, 2001) will repay the diligent reader. "Ethos anthropoi daimon" is usually translated as "character is fate." A more subtle meaning nearer to the author's intent may be "the core of a man is his essence." In Zen, daimon: is the "heart" (Kokoro) essence. In Zen or Taoism, all experience is equivalent for essence; thus no life is wasted and no experience, however "good" or "bad," is futile in advancing enlightenment.

6. Carl Jung (1875-1961), German psychiatrist coined the term "synchronicity" to note that nothing happens by chance. Modern Chaos theory reveals that apparent Chaotic phenomena have underlying order.

7. Shiva "Nata-Raja" "Lord of the Dance of Creation-Destruction" fascinated by the serpent of the world, dancing with his foot on the back of the dwarf "forgetfulness."

8. All negative polarities are underlined by FEARS of . . . . Anticipation, scripting, hope, desire, are all spokes of Samsara's Wheel of Desire – "Attachment". Essence growth occurs at the null point between polarities – "good vs bad" etc.

9. Zazen (Japanese): "Za" (sitting), "Zen" (absorption).

10. The three Greek Eumenides or angry Furies Pursue wrongdoers.

*11. Teilhard de Chardin, SJ (1881-1965) was both a paleoanthropologist who discovered "PeKin" man as well as a Jesuit priest. He formulated the first Christian theory of spiritual evolution of the human soul. Like Darwin before, this was unpopular with the Roman Curia, who sought posthumously to suppress his works. His critical concept was that the collective souls of the church (united in the mystical body of Christ) evolve to higher (more Christ-like) planes of existence and that in doing so, they converge: "**Tout ce monte*** *converge*" (all that rises must converge). Modern complexity theory when applied to consciousness has arrived at the same conclusion. It is impossible to overestimate Teilhard's contribution, but he is, as yet, underappreciated.

12. Blaise Paschal (1623-1662), French mathematician and philosopher once said that philosophical theorizing or religious debate is fine but one must live a life: "If fait juet." One must play (the game). The play action is mediated by "choices" and no-choice is also a choice. This is quintessentially Zen.

13. Marcel Proust, 20th century French writer.

14. A study of the important English translation of the "Tao Te Ching" by Stephen Mitchell (Harper and Row, NY, 1988) will repay the reader.

15. Karma (Sanskrit "deed"): the universal law of cause and effect. "Like attracts Like." Life actions that harm choices engender ribbons that must be cancelled before the debt is paid or essence evolution can occur.

16. The Three Greek Fates: CHLOTHO spins the thread of a life; her sister ATROPOS determines its length and LACHESIS cuts it.

17. Prajna: Sanscrit "consciousness," "wisdom": an immediately experienced initial wisdom that cannot be conveyed by concepts or in intellectual terms. The defining moment of Prajna is insight into emptiness (Sanskrit Shunyata). There is no separate good or evil.

18. Monad: an essential experience which must be learned before essence growth: pursuer – pursued; child – parent;

attacker – victim; etc. The goal of all monads collectively experienced is AGAPE (love without conditions).

19. Seven Essence (and CADENCE) types: server (one), artisan(two), warrior(three), scholar(four), sage(five), priest(six), king(seven).

20. MAYA: Sanskrit: "Illusion" MAYA is the Hindu goddess of Illusion.

21. Lethe: Greek: river crossed from the world of the living to Hades, the world of the Dead. The water of Lethe produces forgetfulness.

22. A study of the spiritual classic: "letters of the Scattered Brotherhood" (Harper, NY, 1948) edited by Mary Strong will repay the reader.

23. Edith Piaf, 20th century French chanteuse speaks for the human condition as does Pascal (12).

24. George Ivanovitch Gurdjieff (1877 – 1949) was a remarkable philosopher-sage who articulated the importance of Centers (intellectual, emotional and moving) in the growth of essence, and the Law of Seven. His student, P.D. Ouspensky (1878 – 1974) was an articulate exponent and teacher of these ideas. Gurdjieff was fascinated by whirling dervishes (Sufi Islamic tradition). "Whirling" occupied and allowed the mind to reach "higher moving center" from which "miraculous enlightenment" can be experienced. Similar "silencing" of the mind by Zazen is also common to Zen, but here higher "intellectual" center is reached. For examples of higher emotional center and enlightenment, see the life and works of St. Teresa of Avila and St. John of the Cross.

25. "The Wallet of Kai Lung" by Ernest Bramah (Dornan Co., N.Y., nd.).

26. Lake Biwa, Japan

27. Mishima Bay, Japan. Seacoast town in sight of Mt. Fuji.

28. Mt. Fuji (Sama, Japanese, "Lord").

29. Lake Ashi, Hakone, Izu Peninsula, Japan. The view of Mt. Fuji up Lake Ashi is one of the most beautiful in Japan.

30. Robert Frost (1874-1963), American poet.
31. Lectio Divina: The Rule of Saint Benedict of Nursia.

32. The Japanese National Theatre for Bunraku, (Puppet Theater) Osaka, Japan. Japanese puppets are life size. It requires thirty years to become Bunraku, "master" or sensei.

33. "Kaigen" the life story of Koichi Tanaka, Japan (2004). Kaigen is the moment the eyes are painted in a work of Buddhist art and when the "Buddha" enters in.

34. Ranier Maria Rilke (1875-1926). Along with Basho, W. B. Yeats, T. S. Elliot, and St. John of the Cross, Rilke was a poet of "innerspace" (innigskeit). A study of the important Rilke translation by Stephen Mitchell will repay the reader. (the Selected Poetry of Ranier Maria Rilke. Edited and translated by Stephen Mitchell (1984) Vintage Books, Random House, New York, N.Y.

Printed in the United States
By Bookmasters